SOCCER TIME!

by Brendan Flynn

BUMBA BOOKS™

LERNER PUBLICATIONS ◆ MINNEAPOLIS

Note to Educators:

Throughout this book, you'll find critical thinking questions. These can be used to engage young readers in thinking critically about the topic and in using the text and photos to do so.

Lerner Publications Company
A division of Lerner Publishing Group, Inc.
241 First Avenue North
Minneapolis, MN 55401 USA

For reading levels and more information, look up this title at www.lernerbooks.com.

Library of Congress Cataloging-in-Publication Data

Names: Flynn, Brendan, 1977–
Title: Soccer time! / by Brendan Flynn.
Description: Minneapolis : Lerner Publications, [2017] | Series: Bumba books—Sports Time! | Includes bibliographical references and index. | Audience: Ages: 4–8. | Audience: Grades: K to Grade 3.
Identifiers: LCCN 2016001058 (print) | LCCN 2016005879 (ebook) | ISBN 9781512414349 (lb : alk. paper) | ISBN 9781512415438 (pb : alk. paper) | ISBN 9781512415445 (eb pdf)
Subjects: LCSH: Soccer—Juvenile literature.
Classification: LCC GV943.25 .F65 2017 (print) | LCC GV943.25 (ebook) | DDC 796.334—dc23

LC record available at http://lccn.loc.gov/2016001058

Manufactured in the United States of America
1 – VP – 7/15/16

Expand learning beyond the printed book. Download free, complementary educational resources for this book from our website, www.lerneresource.com.

Table of Contents

We Play Soccer

Soccer is a fun game.

People play it all over the world.

net

ball

shoes

6

You do not need much to

play soccer.

You need a ball.

You need shoes.

You need a net.

There are two teams.

They play on a grass field.

Each team has a net at one end
of the field.

**Why do the
teams wear
different shirts?**

Players cannot use their hands.

They must kick the ball.

Only the goalie can pick up the ball.

The goalie stands in front of the net.

Why do you think the goalie can pick up the ball?

Players pass the ball to their teammates.

They run down the field.

They try to kick the ball past the goalie.

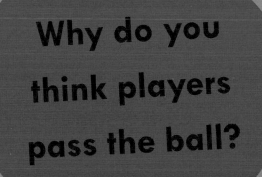

Why do you think players pass the ball?

15

The ball goes into the net!

That is called a goal.

The team with the most

goals wins the game.

You can see a soccer game at your school.

Or your town might have a soccer stadium.

People play soccer all year long.

It is a great sport!

Soccer Field

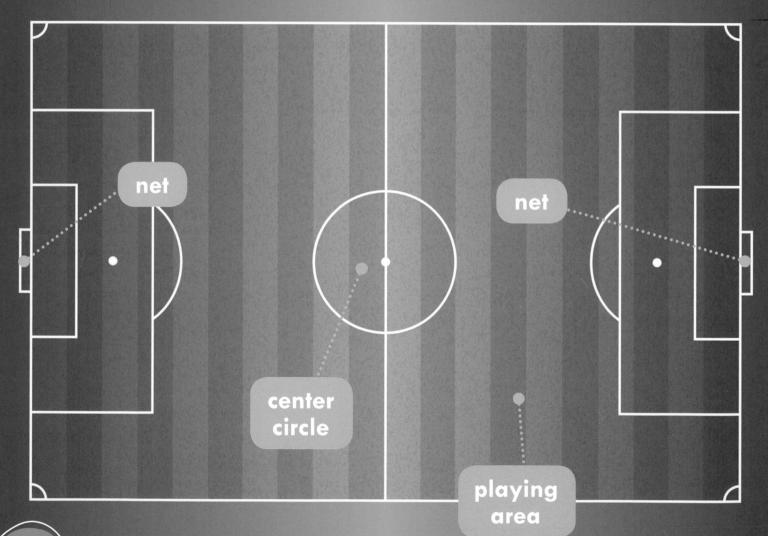

net

net

center circle

playing area

Picture Glossary

goal

when the ball goes into the net

goalie

the player who stops the ball from going into the net

net

the place where players kick the ball to score a goal

pass

to kick the ball to a teammate

Index

Read More

Mattern, Joanne. *I Know Soccer.* Ann Arbor, MI: Cherry Lake Publishing, 2013.

Nagelhout, Ryan. *I Love Soccer.* New York: Gareth Stevens Publishing, 2015.

Nelson, Robin. *Soccer Is Fun!* Minneapolis: Lerner Publications, 2014.

Photo Credits